WALK ULLS & PATTER

TWENTY WALKS AROUI
DOVEDALE, HARTSOP, BROTHERS WATER,
PATTERDALE, GRISEDALE, GLENRIDDING,
ULLSWATER, GLENCOYNE, POOLEY BRIDGE,
FUSEDALE AND MARTINDALE

BILL BIRKETT

BB

BILL BIRKETT PUBLISHING

This book is dedicated to the memory of Jet, my inimitable long haired Border Collie,
with whom I walked all the routes in this guidebook.
And many more besides.

All landscape photographs from the Bill Birkett Photo Library
Maps by Martin Bagness based on pre-1950 Ordnance Survey maps.
Completely redrawn 2020.
Studio photographs of Bill Birkett Guidebooks by
WARD PHOTOGRAPHY 2021.

Book Design by Bill Birkett
Proof Read by Deborah Walsh
Printed in Cumbria by MTP MEDIA
for Bill Birkett Publishing www.billbirkett.com

First published in the UK in 2021.
Copyright © Bill Birkett 2021.
ISBN 978-0-9564296-5-0

DISCLAIMER
Walking in the country and over the fells is potentially dangerous activity and
each individual following the routes described within this book is responsible for
their own safety and actions. Neither the author nor the publisher accepts any
responsibility for the individual safety or actions of anyone using this book. Although the author encountered no difficulty of access on the routes described, and
while considerable effort has been made to avoid so doing, the inclusion of a route
does not imply that a right of way or right of access exists in every case or in all
circumstances. Readers are also advised that changes can occur to the landscape
that may affect the contents of this book. The author welcomes notification of any
such changes.

PHOTOGRAPH CAPTIONS
Front Cover: Over the head of Ullswater from Gowbarrow Fell, Walk 15.
Inside Front Cover: Larch woods above the lower Grisedale Valley, Walk 5.
Back Cover: The White Lion Inn Patterdale in January.
Back Cover: Daffodils by Ullswater in March.
Inside Back Cover: Bill & Jet Birkett, by summit cairn Birkett Fell, Walk 13.
Page [i] Looking over the Kirk Stone towards Patterdale and Place Fell.
Page [iii] Opposite: Looking south over Ullswater's head leg, Walk 14.
Page [iii] Opposite: Helvellyn summit plateau, Walk 9.
Page [vi]: Thornthwaite Beacon, Walk 2.
Page [viii]: Heading for Hartsop, Walk 3.
BOOKENDS ONE: Helvellyn's Striding Edge, Walk 9.
BOOKENDS TWO: Swaledale ewe on Birks, Walk 4.
BOOKENDS THREE: The Grasmere Yearbook.
BOOKENDS FOUR: High Force Waterfall, Walk 14.
BOOKENDS FIVE: North-east down Ullswater middle leg, Walk 14.
BOOKENDS SIX: Bill Birkett Walking Guidebooks.

[ii]

CONTENTS

COLOUR CODE

• = Valley Walk (0 to 200m in altitude)
• = Low Fell Walk (200m to 300m in altitude)
• = Intermediate Fell Walk (300m to 700m in altitude)
• = High Fell Walk (700m to 1000m in altitude)

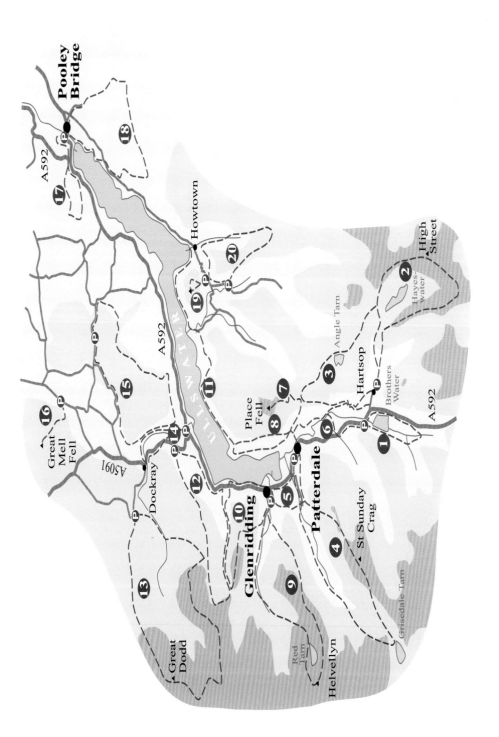

INTRODUCTION

There are twenty walks described in this little guidebook, and one alternative (Walk 20 Over Pikeawassa). Undoubtedly the Ullswater and Patterdale region provides some of the best and most varied walks in the Lake District National Park. Outings that explore a super-lative landscape from lakeside to the lofty heights and which discover numerous secluded and secretive side valleys. From the high adventures on Helvellyn's Striding Edge to the gentle beauty of Ullswater's sylvan shores, the walking here is quite superb.

Patterdale and Ullswater form one long, sinuous valley stretching some 22km from the summit of Kirkstone Pass, at its head, to Pooley Bridge at the foot of Ullswater lake. Three legged Ullswater, some 12km in length and Lakeland's second largest lake, is the major feature of the main valley. The heights to the east are defined by the long whale-back of the High Street ridge, and the skyline to the west by Lakeland's Central Fells: Fairfield, Helvellyn, The Dodds and their ridges. This valley gives perfect access to both areas of fells.

Of the side valleys: first there is Dovedale, overshadowed by mighty Dove Crag perhaps the most formidable of all Lakelands great climbing crags, and bottomed by little Brothers Water. Next there is Hartsop which lies to the east of the main valley, providing a route to Hayeswater and ultimately, the High Street chain of fells. Deepdale ends at Bridgend and my walk through Patterdale Bottom passes through here. Beyond these is the long, deep-sided valley of Grisedale, to the west of Patterdale village. A major valley in itself, it once provided the main packhorse route to Grasmere and the central Lakes. Beyond lies the head of Ullswater and the former mining township of Glenridding. Glenridding Dodd, leading to Sheffield Pike, stands high above the first leg of the three legs of Ullswater and opposite, on the east side of the valley, to the dominant mass of Place Fell.

Before the road leading off to Dockray and above the hidden row of former mine cottages known as Seldom Seen, is the high hanging basin of Glencoyne. Beyond the Dockray Road is the famous Aira Force waterfall and woods at the foot of Gowbarrow Fell. To the east, visible from the heights of Gowbarrow Fell, the dome of Great Mell Fell sits in splendid isolation. To the north of the final leg of Ullswater, above the area known as Waterfoot and Pooley Bridge, are the ancient hillforts of Maiden Castle and Dunmallard Hill.

On the opposite side of the valley, to the south west of Pooley Bridge, stand the heights of Moor Divock. This is an area of particular interest to the archaeologist. Littered with pre-historic remains, most notably The Cockpit Stone Circle, it also marks the north eastern end of the remarkably engineered High Street Roman road.

The quiet, remote, area to the south of the middle leg of Ullswater should not be forgotten. Here, above Howtown Wyke and the lakeshore, stands the distinctive dome of Hallin Fell and, for those who wish to discover hidden gems of the region, the unfrequented valleys of Fusedale, Martindale with its 17th century church, and Boredale.
I have selected twenty circular walks, with the addition of one alternative to Walk 20, for this guidebook. They traverse the heights, the intermediate and low fells, the valleys and some also start in the little villages of Harstop, Patterdale, Glenridding and Pooley Bridge.

[vii]

One of the walks, 'Ullswater's Southern Shore from Glenridding' concludes by making the return to Glenridding from Howtown, by steamer. Furthermore, there are many excellent inns, cafes and places of rest on or nearby all these walks.

There is plenty here for everyone, whether you are an experienced fell walker wishing to scale the heights, or simply want to enjoy the delights of the valley. There are walks and experiences here for all seasons and most weather conditions and by perusing the Fact File, which accompanies each walk description, you can easily select a walk suited to match your ambitions with the prevailing conditions.

Following the immense popularity of 'Walk the Langdales', 'Walk Ambleside, Rydal and Grasmere', 'Walk Windermere and Hawkshead', 'Walk Borrowdale and Keswick' this is the fifth guidebook in the series published by Bill Birkett Publishing. The books are available both locally and nationally through various outlets and bookshops and signed copies are available directly from my website **www.billbirkett.com** (postage free in the UK). Should you forget the guidebook, or choose to use your mobile phone or tablet, downloadable walks are available from my website and they download beautifully and seamlessly to mobile or tablet. Each download features the walk description, map, fact sheet and around a dozen photographs of the walk. Clicking on a highlighted feature takes you straight to a photograph of the feature and then you have the choice to go back to the same text point or the map. Simple and effective - give it a try.

USING THIS GUIDE
The format of this guide is simple and straightforward. Overall maps, on the back cover and within the contents page (page v), show immediately where the individual walks lie. Each numbered walk is described on a double page spread, you don't need to turn the page mid walk, with a suitably detailed map that can form the basis of the walk (although it is recommended that you also take an OS map with you for detailed reference and navigation, particularly on the high fells). My photographs illustrate some highlights and capture the general ambiance of the walk. The Fact File provides the essential information and identifies places to eat, drink, rest, shelter on each individual walk. Colour coded on the Contents Page, are classification of the walks as; Valley (0 to 200m in altitude), Low Fell (200m to 300m), Intermediate Fell (300m to 700m), High Fell (700m to 1000m). The ring-binding keeps the guidebook flat in your pocket and always allows it to open on the page of your chosen walk.

CAUTION
Particularly on the fells it is important that walkers have equipment suitable for both prevailing and possible conditions. Suitable footwear, weatherproof clothing, map and compass or GPS, are essential requirements. For guidance on navigation, clothing and foowear in both summer and winter, survival and tips on photography, see 'The Hillwalker's Manual' by Bill Birkett.

WALK 1
A CIRCUIT OF BROTHERS WATER

At the foot of Kirkstone Pass, nestling in the narrow head of the long Ullswater Valley, Brothers Water's dark mirror reflects many different moods. This easy clockwise circuit extends to pass Hartsop Hall and continues through an impressively located ancient settlement. Footbridges over three becks then lead to the road from where a permissive path leads past the Brotherswater Inn and on beside the east shore of Brothers Water.

THE ROUTE

Follow the track through the wonderful oak woods above the western shore of the lake. Pass the interesting buildings of Hartsop Hall and bear right. Before the barns and outbuildings go left and take the gate leading into the field.

◆ Follow the grassy track across the

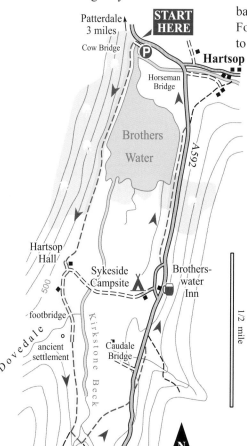

field and take the stone slab bridge over Dovedale Beck. Pass through a Prehistoric Settlement set amidst dramatic mountain scenery. It is marked by piles of stones, raised earthworks and huge boulders standing to a height of   2.5m. Continue along the grassy track to pass in front of a barn. Bear left to traverse above the wall. Follow the path until, as it begins to rise up to Scandale Pass, a lesser path drops off to the left to cross little Caiston Beck by a wooden footbridge.

◆ Walk by the wall then left through the gate to cross Kirkstone Beck by the footbridge which is followed by a flat wooden bridge over a stream. Keep straight on then bear right around the drumlins. Gain the little path beneath the stone wall bounding the Kirkstone Pass Road and bear left to follow it rising to a gate. Go left along the road rounding the bend to a widening. At this point cross over to take a signed footpath running above the road. The path drops to cross a footbridge alongside Caudale Bridge. Rise with the path until it falls to join the road. Bear right to the Brotherswater Inn.

◆ Continue along   below the inn and then take the surfaced drive on the right. This leads to a narrow permisssive path leading off left.

◆ Follow the path, below the road and then along just above the shore of the lake (if flooded ascend to the road).

◆ Continue across the meadows until forced out right onto the road once

WALK 1

Looking south west over Brothers Water into Dovedale, viewed from the east shore path.

On top of a boulder in the ancient settlement.

more. Go left and follow the wide verge beside the road until, over Horseman Bridge and opposite the junction to Hartsop and the bus shelter, cross over to follow the pavement beside the road. Cross the road again to return to Cow Bridge car park.

FACT FILE

CLASS: *Valley Walk (max alt 200m).*
LENGTH: 6 km.
TIME: 2 hours.
DIFFICULTY: Easy, though can be boggy below the Kirkstone Pass.

START & FINISH: Cow Bridge car park Hartsop (402 134).
MAPS: OS L90 or OL5.
HOSTELRIES: Brotherswater Inn enroute.

WALK 2
HIGH STREET BY THE HAYESWATER HORSESHOE

Little Hayeswater nestles in the high hills above the village of Hartsop with it's anticlock-wise circumnavigation, described here, forming a natural mountain horseshoe. The way, generally grassy and straightforward, includes a section of trackway first engineered by the Romans; the famous High Street Roman Road. Its northern leg rises by The Knott and along the Straits of Riggindale to traverse, or summit, the mighty fell of High Street. Its southern leg descends by Thornthwaite Beacon and Gray Crag returning to the stone cottages of Hartsop.

THE ROUTE

Take the gate at the head of the car park and follow the track left of the sheep pens. Cross the bridge over Hayeswater Gill and ascend the track, passing the traditional stone barn. Keep climbing until a footbridge to the left re-crosses the gill a little below Hayeswater.

◆ Rise with the path, the tarn becomes

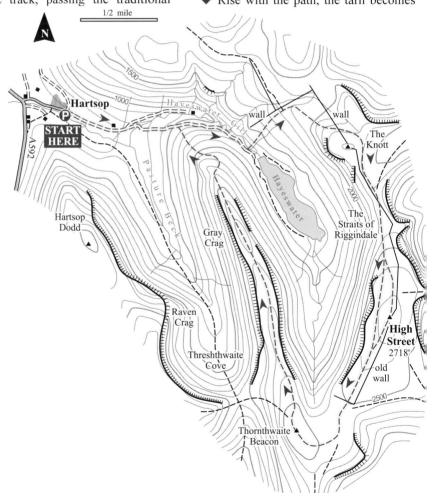

Looking from Gray Crag over the head of Hayeswater towards High Street.

visible to the right, making direct ascent up the steep grassy hillside. Boggy in places. At the levelling the path joins a stone wall and a well defined path by the gap. Bear right along the path and make ascent up the steepening flanks of The Knott. The easiest path traverses left around the summit knoll and then back right to gain the line of a stone wall. Follow this and then make descent into the dip along the section of track known as The Straits of Riggindale.

◆ After a short section of ascent the easiest route, with fine views over the Hayeswater basin, bears right to follow a well defined track. Possibly the original line of High Street Roman Road. (Alternatively follow the track continuing along the line of the stone wall making ascent to gain the summit of High Street.) Keep right along the track and traverse around the rim of the basin until a short ascent leads to the high stone tower which marks the summit of Thornthwaite Beacon.

◆ Follow the wall north then bear right along the path to follow the grassy path first in descent then making slight ascent along to the cairned end of Gray Crag. Follow the path down the nose of the fell until nearing its base, with the original lower track in sight, the way goes first right, to avoid a steep crag, before doubling back left below the rocks. The grassy path heads for a stone wall then drops rightwards making steep descent to regain the original track. At this point there stands a large boulder bedecked with a little cairn. Descend to the car park.

FACT FILE

CLASS: *High Fell Walk (max alt 828m).*
LENGTH: *11¼ km*
TIME: *4½ hours.*
DIFFICULTY: *A difficult mountain route (762m of ascent).*

START & FINISH: *Car park at end of Hartsop village (410 130).*
MAPS: *OS L90 or OL5.*
HOSTELRIES: *Brotherswater Inn nearby.*

WALK 3

ANGLE TARN FROM HARTSOP BY HAYESWATER AND BOREDALE HAUSE

A fine anticlockwise outing visiting one of Lakeland's most sublime mountain tarns. There are superb views throughout. A track leads to the foot Hayeswater from where a steep grassy ascent gains a very good path. This path traverses a high shoulder first to Angle Tarn and then on to the pass of Boredale Hause. From here a track falls to the Patterdale valley before rising slightly to traverse back to the village of Hartsop. Overlooking Angle Tarn the two tops of the Angletarn Pikes may be included for little extra effort.

THE ROUTE

Take the gate at the head of the car park and follow the track left of the sheep pens. Cross the bridge over Hayeswater Gill and ascend the track, passing the traditional stone barn. Keep climbing until a footbridge to the left re-crosses the gill a little below Hayeswater. Rise with the path, the tarn becomes visible to the right, making direct ascent up the steep grassy hillside. Boggy in places. At the levelling the path joins a stone wall and a well defined path by the gap.

◆ Go left and follow the well defined path which continues to skirt just below the crest of the shoulder before falling to Angle Tarn.

◆ Continue along the path to skirt around beneath the heights of Angletarn Pikes. (Alternatively bear right to make an ascent of the South Pike and then cross to the North Pike before returning by a steep but short descent back to the main path.) The path descends a little grasssy corridor before bearing left to the pass of Boredale Hause.

◆ Descend leftwards along the main track to reach Patterdale valley. Bear left and continue along the level track, passing the ruined barns of Dubhow, followed by a short footbridge crossing the gill until reaching the waterfalls of Angletarn Beck. There are two bridges.

◆ Cross the higher wooden footbridge and keep along the path to pass between two houses perched on the hillside. Go up and left along the track until it descends back to

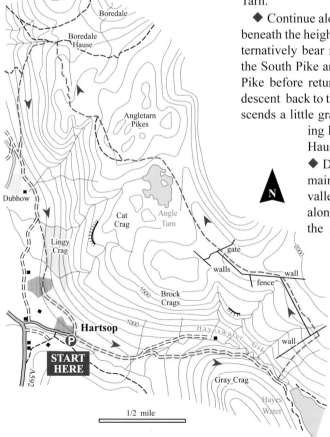

WALK 3

Looking over Angle Tarn from Angletarn PIkes.

Hartsop Village. Turn left along road to the car park.

Seen right of Place Fell, the pass of Boredale Hause.

Returning to Hartsop Village.

FACT FILE

CLASS: *Intermediate Fell Walk (max alt 567m).*
LENGTH: *9½ km.*
TIME: : *3½ hours.*
DIFFICULTY: *A mildly difficult route*

(570m of ascent).
START & FINISH: *Car park at end of Hartsop village (410 130).*
MAPS: *OS L90 or OL5.*
HOSTELRIES: *Brotherswater Inn nearby.*

WALK 4

THE GRISEDALE AND ST SUNDAY CRAG CIRCUIT FROM PATTERDALE

On this walk the heights are gained by gradual ascent, first by slowly climbing the Grisedale Valley to Grisedale Tarn, then by traversing the hillside diagonally to gain the gentle summit shoulder leading to the top of St Sunday Crag. Equally affable in descent an excellent path leads across the northern flanks of Birks, with tremendous views over the head of Ullswater, to drop to valley level and return to Patterdale. One of the finest outings to be had in the Lakeland fells.

THE ROUTE

From Patterdale Hotel car park head north through the village. Pass the church until the road 'Lane to Grisedale' branches off left. Ascend the road until it levels and enters the level Grisedale valley.

◆ At the junction take the surfaced road to the right to cross the bridge over Grisedale Beck. Climb the hill and continue directly through the gate and up the steep field. Take the high gate on the left and then follow the path above and parallel to the stone wall. Keep along this path all the way up the north side of the scenic mountain valley of Grisedale. Continue in ascent to pass the ruined building beneath Eagle Crag's old mines and continue to a footbridge and junction with the south-side valley path to

bear right and ascend to the building of Ruthwaite Lodge.

◆ Continue climbing the stony path to a large cairn. Bear left to the foot of Grisedale Tarn and cross the beck via the stepping stones.

◆ Immediately head left and follow the narrow diagonal pass rising across the hillside. Near its end it zigzags sharply and

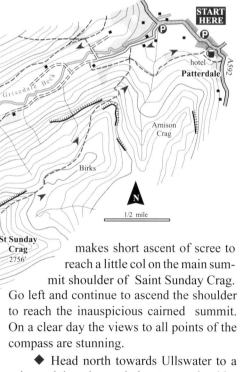

makes short ascent of scree to reach a little col on the main summit shoulder of Saint Sunday Crag. Go left and continue to ascend the shoulder to reach the inauspicious cairned summit. On a clear day the views to all points of the compass are stunning.

◆ Head north towards Ullswater to a cairn and then descend the steeper shoulder below. As the going levels, in a little hollow below the grassy shoulder of Birks, a narrow

The high peak of St Sunday Crag seen over the head of Ullswater, the Grisedale valley to its right.

but well defined path leads off leftwards.

◆ Follow this path across the grassy north flanks of Birks, with wonderful views over the head of Ullswater, until a steep descent leads to a little gate through a stone wall.

Across the north flanks of Birks.

◆ Immediately head left and descend the path and stone steps all the way to a junction with the path at valley level by the large oak trees. The gate below the path leads more directly to the playing field but for the main car park in Patterdale bear right. Follow the path all way until it drops to a little wood. Enter the wood and bear left to pass the Patterdale Hotel.

FACT FILE

CLASS: *High Fell Walk (max alt 841m).*
LENGTH: *14 km.*
TIME: *6 hours.*
DIFFICULTY: *A long, difficult mountain route on good paths (825m of ascent).*

START & FINISH: *Car park opposite Patterdale Hotel (396 159). Or Playing Field (390 160).*
MAPS: *OS L90 or OL5.*
HOSTELRIES: *Plentiful in Patterdale.*

WALK 5

LANTY'S TARN, KELDAS AND GLENRIDDING FROM PATTERDALE

A very pleasant and relatively short clockwise circuit from Patterdale. It crosses the foot of the Grisedale Valley to offer a mix of trees, traditional stone buildings including the Thornthwaite Barn, the delightful and secretive little Lanty's Tarn, the summit of Keldas overlooking Ullswater, the delights of Glenridding, and the boats and boathouses around the head of Ulllswater. Fine and varied views throughout.

THE ROUTE

Pass the north end of the Patterdale Hotel to find a little path which leads right through the cluster of birch to a kissing gate. An open track rises rightwards to traverse the hillside above the stone wall. Open views extend over Ullswater and there are many fine trees with a mixture of apple and thorn blossom in springtime.

◆ Pass through a gate and keep along the well defined track. Cross the stepping stones over Hag Beck, to contour around the hillside and enter a wood of tall, ancient larch. Continue, until some little stone enclosures stand against the hillside to the left and a gate on the right leads down through the fields to the old stone barn of Thornhow. Follow down the track, bear right and then left along the surfaced road, to cross the fine stone arch bridge over Grisedale Beck.

◆ Climb the lane and keep straight on to go through the gate and steeply climb the field. Take the lower gate on the right to emerge through the fell wall. Go right along the level grassy track for 100m then climb steeply leftwards to skirt the reclusive Lanty Tarn.

◆ Beyond the tarn a path leads down the hillside, eventually falling to the buildings of Westside. However, a worthwhile diversion can first be made by turning right, beyond the kissing gate which leaves the tarn, to follow the path to the summit of Keldas.

◆ Return to the original path then continue the descent to pass Westside and on to the banks of Glenridding Beck. Bear right to reach main road in Glenridding.

◆ Go right and follow the road to Patterdale. By the lake a permissive path keeps right above the road and St. Patrick's Well only to rejoin the road and cross to the other side to divert through the trees for a short way. Continue taking the roadside pavements to pass the church and return to the Patterdale Hotel.

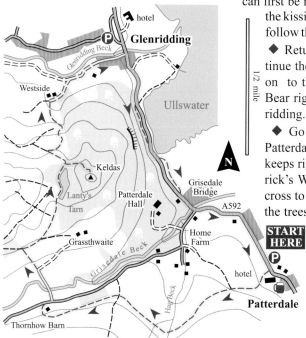

WALK 5

Thornhow Barn.

Lanty Tarn.

FACT FILE

CLASS: *Low Fell Walk (max alt 311m).*
LENGTH: 5 km.
TIME: 3 hours.
DIFFICULTY: Moderately difficult, mainly on good paths (265m of ascent).

START & FINISH:Car park opposite Patterdale Hotel (396 159).
MAPS: OS L90 or OL5.
HOSTELRIES: Plentiful in Patterdale and Glenridding.

WALK 6
PATTERDALE VALLEY BOTTOM

Exploring the many different facets of Patterdale this is an easy valley walk, suitable for all seasons. Proceeding in clockwise mode, cross the bridge over Goldrill Beck and continue through the stone cottages and farms of Rooking, Crookabeck, Beckstones, Dubhow and Hartsop on the east side of the valley. On the west side of the dale make return from Cow Bridge through Low Wood and the hamlet of Bridgend, to cross the meadows and regain the original lane upstream of Beckstones.

THE ROUTE

Head west from the car park and pass through the narrows of the village then go left over the bridge crossing Goldrill Beck. Follow the surfaced lane to Rooking and at the junction go right. Keep along the lane to the hamlet of Crookabeck and pass through the buildings to continue along the lane. This rises to traverse through

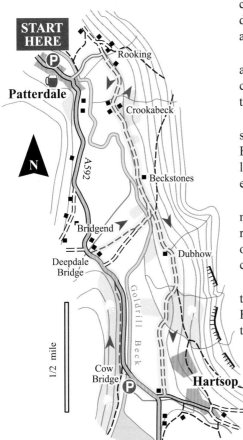

wonderful oakwoods before passing by the farmstead of Beckstones.

◆ Keep along the lane to take the left branch at the first junction. Follow the lane, keeping right to pass the intersection of the Boredale Hause track. Descend slightly to pass the ruins of Dubhow farmstead, seen over the stone wall to the right. Continue to cross a stony beck (wooden footbridge seldom used), and continue to the larger beck, and tumbling waterfalls of Angletarn Beck.

◆ Cross the beck on the lower footbridge and keep along the lane all the way to intercept the road entering Hartsop. Go right to the main road (bus-stop and shelter).

◆ Go right along the road until it is possible to cross left to the car park at Cow Bridge. Cross the stone bridge to see, directly ahead a little gate (beside the iron bench) entering Low Wood.

◆ Through the gate go right along the narrow footpath through the woods which runs parallel to the main road. Emerge onto the wide verge and follow this to cross the road bridge of Deepdale Bridge.

◆ Immediately go right crossing the road to follow the lane through the hamlet of Bridgend. Take the path across the meadows to join the track leading to a bridge over the main beck - Godrill Beck. A short rise leads back to the original track and on in a short way to the farmstead of Beckstones. Retrace your steps returning to Patterdale village.

WALK 6

The lane to Rooking.

Bridgend.

FACT FILE

CLASS: *Valley Walk (max alt 180m).*
LENGTH: 8 km.
TIME: 2½ hours.
DIFFICULTY: Easy, mainly level going
(175m of ascent).

START & FINISH: *Car park opposite*
Patterdale Hotel (396 159).
MAPS: OS L90 or OL5.
HOSTELRIES: Plentiful in Patterdale.

WALK 7
PLACE FELL FROM PATTERDALE

Rising directly from the eastern shoreline of Ullswater, located in the crook of its top two legs, Place Fell is the most visibly dominant fell in the whole of the Patterdale/Ullswater valley. It's most straightforward ascent, described here, begins from Patterdale and climbs first to Boredale Hause and then by way of its southern shoulder, passing by Round How, to gain the rock summit knoll. Both in ascent and descent, and from its plucky top knot, the views are superb.

THE ROUTE

Head west from the car park and walk through the narrows of the village, then go left over the bridge crossing Goldrill Beck. Follow the surfaced lane to Rooking and at the junction go left. Go up the road until the high gate on the right leads to open fellside.

◆ Keep right - there are two well defined tracks which split into higher and lower. Take the highest track leading rightwards to pass the iron bench -'18VR97'. These sturdy benches commemoratiiong Queen Victoria's Diamond Jubilee are dotted all round the area - see how many you can find. The diagonal ascent is unmistakeable and, after re-joining the lower path, a little further ascent leads to a broader track. Ascend to a flatish area with a ruinous rectangular stone structure to the right, over the little stream. This is an old washfold and predates chemical dipping of the sheep.

◆ At the level area don't take the first path left but climb a little further to find another vague grassy path heading off to the left. The actual grassy summit area of Boredale Hause lies beyond this but we don't go that far. The vague path rounds a little grassy rise and passes the end of a ruinous stone rectangular structure- this is the so called 'Chapel in the Hause'.

◆ Immediately the vague path becomes a well defined track which continues leftwards at first, towards the edge of the hillside, before bearing

off right. It then zags steeply back leftwards to the edge of the fell once again. This is Steel Edge and affords good views over the valley below.

◆ After a short ascent the way leads rightwards to make a rocky scramble up a short ravine to gain the top of the distinct rocky knoll known as Round How. From here the going eases and undulates along the summit shoulder until the rocky summit knoll and trig point of Place Fell stand to the right. Wonderful position and magnificent views.

◆ Follow the same route in descent with the exception that it is better to pass Round How on the right, missing the ravine. Down the track below below Boredale Hause the lower diagonal track can be taken for the sake of variety.

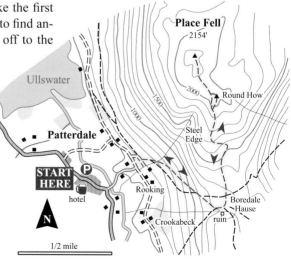

WALK 7

Place Fell from Glenridding.

Looking NE over Place Fell summit trig. point.

FACT FILE

CLASS: *High Fell Walk (max alt 657m).*
LENGTH: *6¾ km.*
TIME: *3 hours.*
DIFFICULTY: *Difficult, generally straight-forward (535m of ascent).*

START & FINISH: *Car park opposite Patterdale Hotel (396 159).*
MAPS: *OS L90 or OL5.*
HOSTELRIES: *Plentiful in Patterdale.*

WALK 8
SILVER POINT FROM PATTERDALE

An entertaining walk with fine views throughout, this excellent and straightforward circuit reaches out from Patterdale village to one of Ullswater's most famed viewpoints - Silver Point. Above Rooking a high traverse, along an excellent, narrow, constructed path/track, by old slates quarries, leads to Silver Crag. A short descent then gains Silver Point which protrudes strategically between the top two legs of Ullswater. Lakeside return leads to Side Farm and then along the riverbank back to Patterdale Bridge.

THE ROUTE

Head west from the car park and walk through the narrows of the village, then go left over the bridge crossing Goldrill Beck. Follow the surfaced lane to Rooking and at the junction go left. Go up the road until the high gate on the right leads to open fellside.

◆ Beyond the gate cross the flat concrete bridge and rise above the stone built Placefell Cottage until a path leads off to the left. Follow this path, undulating only slightly, to pass two slate quarry workings until finally rising to the corridor right of the distinct craggy knoll of Silver Crag.

◆ Descend the path and stone steps, rough in places, to gain the level path. Go left along the path to gain the neck of Silver Point. Various rock hummocks provide picnic points and fine views.

◆ Regain the path and head south along the stone path, towards the head of the lake, to rise slightly to the rocky knoll bedecked with Scots Pine. Continue along the track through woods and by the stone wall to enter the buildings of Side Farm.

◆ Midway through the farm turn right and follow the driveway track to the bridge over Goldrill Beck. Turn left before crossing and follow the river bank back to the surfaced lane. Go right over Patterdale Bridge and back to the starting point.

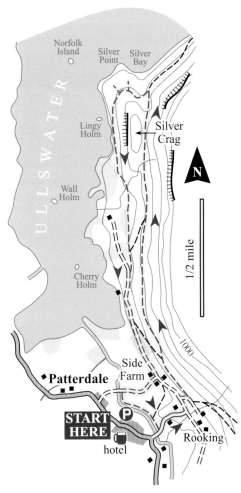

WALK 8

The high path to Silver Crag, looking across the head of Ullswater.

The low track which returns to Side Farm.
Opposite: On Silver Point.

FACT FILE

CLASS: *Valley Walk (max alt 248m).*
LENGTH: 6¾ km.
TIME: 2½ hours.
DIFFICULTY: Easy, on well defined paths
(244m of ascent).

START & FINISH:Car park opposite
Patterdale Hotel (396 159).
MAPS: OS L90 or OL5.
HOSTELRIES: Plentiful in Patterdale.

WALK 9

HELVELLYN BY THE RED TARN HORSESHOE – UP STRIDING EDGE AND DOWN SWIRRAL EDGE.

This famous horseshoe rises from Glenridding and traverses Striding Edge to gain the summit of Helvellyn before making descent via Swirral Edge. One of the most popular summer walks in the Lake District it should not be underestimated. Striding Edge is a sharp rocky ridge requiring a head for heights and some scrambling ability. Descent of Swirral Edge is also very exposed, steep and eroded. A successful traverse of this great horseshoe is a feather in anyone's cap - but have a care, know your abilities and assess the conditions carefully.

THE ROUTE

Gain and the road which rises through Glenridding village to pass The Travellers Rest Inn and on to a junction at the bend. Bear left to cross Glenridding Beck by Rattlebeck Bridge. Climb the stony track with Mires Beck down to the left. Beyond a gate follow the main track to ascend by zagging first left and then right before rising to the wall. A ladder stile and gate lead to open fellside. Follow the path, bearing left to cross Mires Beck, and ascend the left bank, climbing up Little Cove to gain a stone wall running down from the shoulder above.

◆ Initially the main path leads up by wall before, nearing the top of the shoulder, it sweeps to the right finally climbing to the grassy ridge. Proceed along the shoulder to regain the line of the wall and follow it to pass a stile down to the left, known as the Hole-in-the-Wall. Beyond the wall ascend the shoulder to traverse Low Spying How before gaining High Spying How - the rocky end cone of Striding Edge.

◆ Following the undulating rocky crest of Striding Edge is airy and a little scrambly. A number of rises are crested before the final tower which terminates the edge proper. Descent from this, down a steep little gully towards the south side, presents the most difficult section.

◆ Once down, cross the gap in the ridge to gain a small rocky buttress. A little mild

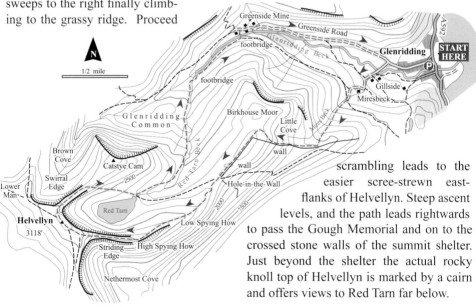

scrambling leads to the easier scree-strewn east-flanks of Helvellyn. Steep ascent levels, and the path leads rightwards to pass the Gough Memorial and on to the crossed stone walls of the summit shelter. Just beyond the shelter the actual rocky knoll top of Helvellyn is marked by a cairn and offers views to Red Tarn far below.

WALK 9

Striding Edge viewed from Helvellyn's summit plateau, Red Tarn nestles in the basin beyond.

◆ Follow the curving rim of the summit plateau past the trig point and on to the top of Swirral Edge. The path seems to plunge into an abyss and looks impossibly steep. Take heart, although exposed, it isn't quite as bad as it looks and the going eases rapidly after the first section of descent. Continue descending the ridge until the going levels then take the path descending diagonally rightwards towards the outfall of Red Tarn.

◆ Keep along the well defined path which descends into the head of Glenridding. Cross Red Tarn Beck by a little footbridge and keep along the path above Glenridding Beck until it is crossed by a footbridge. Cross the bridge and proceed down the track, passing the old mine buildings (now a Youth Hostel) to gain the Greenside Road. Decend the road and continue passed the traditional Inn of the Travellers Rest en-route to the car park.

Helvellyn summit shelter.

FACT FILE	
CLASS: *High Fell Walk (max alt 950m).*	START & FINISH:*Glenridding car park*
LENGTH: *12 km.*	*(NY 385 169).*
TIME: *5½ hours.*	MAPS: *OS L90 or OL5.*
DIFFICULTY: *A very difficult high mountain route (894m of ascent).*	HOSTELRIES: *Plentiful in Glenridding.*

WALK 10
SHEFFIELD PIKE FROM GLENRIDDING RETURNING BY SELDOM SEEN AND ULLSWATER

Sheffield Pike rises directly behind the village of Glenridding. Along with its little outlier, Glenridding Dodd, its ascent offers fine views over Ullswater to the eastern fells and also up to Helvellyn and The Dodds. Starting from Glenridding this route climbs steeply up The Rake to first gain Glenridding Dodd then climbs by Heron Pike to reach the summit of Sheffield Pike. Descent leads to Nick Head and then down Glencoyne to pass the cottages of Seldon Seen before continuing to lake level. A delightful traverse by the western shores of Ullswater leads back to Glenridding.

THE ROUTE

From the car park gain the road rising through the houses of Glenridding to pass The Travellers Rest Inn. Go round the bends and rise with the road to pass the first set of cottages standing above to the right. Continue along the road to a cattle grid. Go right and climb a grassy path which soon steepens to rise to the left of Blaes Crag. The main path goes left to make a steep ascent of the hillside - The Rake. At the stone wall take the path running right. After a short way a path moves off climbing right to the independent top of Glenridding Dodd.

Return, descending to the low point of the stone wall.

◆ Rise with the wall to find a gap to the right. Go right and follow the little path above the wall which leads across the hillside beneath Heron Pike. Before a craggy knoll ascend, away from the wall, towards the craggy face of Heron Pike. A narrow grassy path rises up the stepped shoulder to the right. Climb the shoulder keeping to the right of the pinnacle and craggy face of Heron Pike. As the going begins to level the path becomes better defined and leads across the shoulder to the cairned summit of Sheffield Pike. A

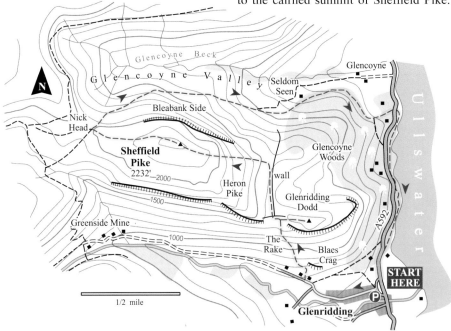

WALK 10

Looking to Heron Pike and Sheffield Pike above Glenridding.

commanding position with extensive views.

◆ From the summit make descent of the west shoulder to the col, known as Nick Head. Take the path leading down right into the head of the Glencoyne valley. The path contours rightwards and makes a surprisingly easy descent across the northern flank, known as Bleabank Side, of Sheffield Pike. A little gate leads through the fell wall. Pass through the gate and follow the path descending parallel to the stone wall which runs along the south side of the Glencoyne Valley. The path steepens, passes between two large boulders, and continues to a junction of walls. Keep straight on, over the wooden stile, to enter the woods. Follow the path above the wall to pass the cottages of Seldom Seen and reach a little track. Descend to gain the main road.

◆ Cross the road with care to find, on the left end of a little stone boundary wall, a path running below. Go right along the path and follow it to a point where it reaches the lakeshore. Beyond lies the rock cutting of Stybarrow Crag. Join and follow the road for a little way until a path opens through the trees to the left. Follow the path until steps climb up to the right. Climb the little hill, viewpoint, and descend again until finally the path rejoins the road. Continue along the pavement back to the car park.

FACT FILE

CLASS: *Intermediate Fell Walk (max alt 675m).*
LENGTH: *8¼ km.*
TIME: *4½ hours.*
DIFFICULTY: *Difficult, good paths prevail*

(625m of ascent).
START & FINISH:Glenridding car park (NY 385 169).
MAPS: OS L90 or OL5.
HOSTELRIES: Plentiful in Glenridding.

WALK 11
ULLSWATER'S SOUTHERN SHORE FROM GLENRIDDING

Nestling beneath the fells all the radiant beauty and sylvan serenity of Lake Ullswater are encompassed on this outstanding walk. A linear outing, starting from Glenridding, rounding the head of Ullswater and continuing to Howtown to return by steamer. The going is relatively easy throughout and this, combined with its relatively low level, make the walk attractive to a wide range of abilities. A 40 minute boat trip makes a return, in great style and with no effort, to Glenridding.

THE ROUTE

With its head and south shore dominated by steep fells, the three legs of Ullswater lead north eastwards from the central fells to the open plains beyond. This walk rounds the head of the lake before following the south shore along its middle leg, to offer a walk of outstanding natural beauty. Returning by steamer is part of the fun of the outing. Regular sailings occur daily throughout the year but consult the current timetable before starting.

◆ From Glenridding follow the road, and roadside paths, south to Patterdale. Turn left along the lane which leads to Side Farm. Through the farm turn left and follow the main track. Continue at a low level,

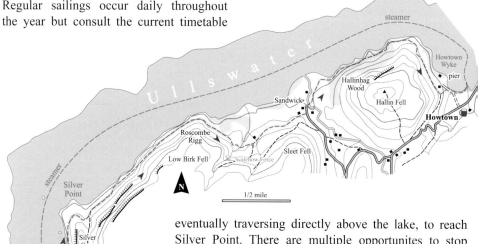

eventually traversing directly above the lake, to reach Silver Point. There are multiple opportunites to stop and enjoy the view.

◆ Keep along the narrow but well-defined path above the lake until, at Roscombe Rigg, the path moves away from the lake above Scalehow Wood. Cross the footbridge over Scalehow Beck (waterfall above best viewed beyond the bridge), and continue along the track, passing Lowther Barn Tearoom, to the hamlet of Sandwick. Go left, then right, to cross the bridge over Sandwick Beck.

◆ Continue to reach and then traverse the shoreline by the oaks of Hallinhag Wood. The path rounds the headland of Hallin Fell to continue above Howtown Wyke Bay to the buildings of Waternook. Bear left down to the shore and continue directly to the steamer pier.

WALK 11

The path heading for Silver Point.

The steamer awaits in Howtown Wyke.

FACT FILE

CLASS: *Lakeside Walk (max alt 208m).*
LENGTH: *10½ km.*
TIME: *3½ hours.*
DIFFICULTY: *Easy (420m of ascent).*
START & FINISH: *Glenridding car park*

(NY 385 169).
MAPS: OS L90 or OL5.
HOSTELRIES: Plentiful in Glenridding,
Side Farm Tearoom, Lowther Barn Tea-
room, Howtown Tearoom & Hotel Bar.

WALK 12
A ROUND OF GLENCOYNE

Above the western shore of Ullswater, the hanging basin of Glencoyne nestles high in the fells above Glencoyne Farm. This route starts high on Park Brow to traverse through the oakwoods of Gencoyne Park before rising through the ancient beech above Bell Knot to gain the grassy shoulder of Brown Hills. From here the circuit around the natural mountain amphitheatre of Glencoyne Head is virtually horizontal in execution despite its spectacular position. Nick Head leads to descent via the miner's stone cottages of Seldom Seen then to the farm of Glencoyne before reaching lake level. A path through oakwoods and open fields leads back to Park Brow. An outing of great character with a tremendous aspect over Ullswater lake.

THE ROUTE

Just below the car park, on the opposite of the road, stands a sign and stile. Take the narrow well defined path leading through the woods. Cross the rift of Groove Gill to a gate in the stone wall. Rise through the mighty trees above Bell Knott which open to reveal stunning views.

◆ A grassy zigzag track rises steeply to pass through a stone wall and gain the grassy shoulder of Brown Hills.

◆ Head easily left and take the gap in the wall to continue traversing around the basin. The hillside is steep but the narrow path good and well defined. Cross the ravine of Wintergroove Gill and continue around the basin, above mine workings, to make gradual ascent up the rocky path until a grassy shoulder drops to Nick Head.

◆ Descend the nick and follow the path traversing

the hillside before dropping to follow along above the stone wall.

◆ Just before the wood take the gate on the left and descend the broad grassy path to pass below the low building beneath the Seldom Seen row of cottages. A grassy track leads to Glencoyne Farm. Go right, through the back garden of the farmhouse (signed right of way) and continue down the track towards the road.

◆ Go left along the path beside the road to pass through the car park and pass over a wooden footbridge. Continue through the oaks just above the road. A little gate and

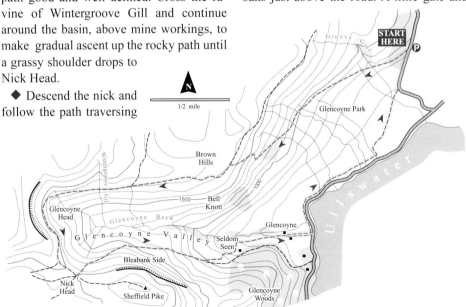

The aspect from Spying How by Bell Knot.

To Glencoyne Head.

wooden footbridge lead to a track.

◆ Ascend the track, away from the road, to the fence and then go right to a gate. Go through this gate and continue beside the fence to pass through an opening and bear left to cross a wooden footbridge. Cross the hummocky rough field and ascend to the little wooden gate leading onto the road rising up Park Brow.

FACT FILE

CLASS: *Intermediate Fell Walk (max alt 613m).*
LENGTH: *10¾ km.*
TIME: *5 hours.*
DIFFICULTY: *Mildly Difficult on good paths (575m of ascent).*

START & FINISH: *NT Car Park beside Dockray Road (NY 398 206).*
MAPS: *OS L90 or OL5.*
HOSTELRIES: *The Royal Hotel Dockray & Aira Force Tearoom nearby.*

WALK 13
BIRKETT FELL AND THE DODDS HORSESHOE

Beginning by the end of the Old Coach Road the way leads first to Dowthwaitehead then by grassy paths over Birkett Fell to rise via Hart Side and White Stones. Then summiting Stybarrow Dodd it continues to make a horseshoe around The Dodds before dropping by Randerside and back to the Coach Road. Though it can be boggy in the lower sections this is a pleasant outing with great views from the tops. Birkett Fell - a good name!

THE ROUTE

Beginning and ending by the end of the Old Coach Road this is a straightforward high fell outing. Walk along the road to the cluster of farms at Dowthwaitehead.

◆ Pass through the buildings to exit on the lane to the left. Bear right at the barn and cross the footbridge to ascend beside the wall. Continue to ascend by the grassy path, vague in places and often boggy. Pass through the gap in the wall and ascend to a prominent kissing gate and signpost.

◆ Continue the diagonal ascent to gain the distinct stone wall and take the stile (or gap) then follow the left side of the wall until a path branches off left to the cairned top of Birkett Fell.

◆ The grassy path/track continues along the shoulder until a path leads rightwards to ascend the bump of Hart Side. Descend the grassy path leading in the direction of White Stones. Either top out on Hart Side or keep traversing the easier path on its right side. Steeper ascent leads up the grassy bump of Stybarrow Dodd. A small cairn stands to the left and a tiny tarn in front (sometimes dry).

◆ Go over the top and down to the grassy shoulder. Head left out to the cairned top of Watson's Dodd (fine views). Head back right and ascend the final grassy mound of Great Dodd passing a large stone shelter structure before reaching the summit cairn.

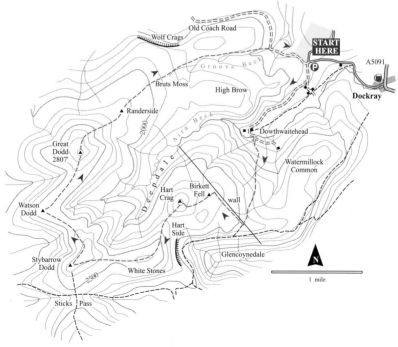

Dowthwaitehead.

On Great Dodd looking north west.

◆ Bear right to find a small cairn on the edge of the plateau and then descend the obvious grassy path which leads to the cloven-hoof point of Randerside. The right-hand protuberance is the highest point.

◆ Regain the central path and descend by the delights of Bruts Moss and Whams Moss, to keep to the right of the grassy hill. The route is obvious, though often it is impossible to find a dry way. The track improves above Groove Beck and leads down to the Old Coach Road. Head right, either fording the stream or taking the footbridge, back along the track to the start.

FACT FILE

CLASS: *High Fell Walk (max alt 857m).*
LENGTH: *14 km.*
TIME: *4½ hours.*
DIFFICULTY: *Difficult, on grassy paths though can be boggy (575m of ascent).*

START & FINISH: *By road junction (NY 380 219).*
MAPS: *OS L90 or OL5.*
HOSTELRIES: *The Royal Hotel Dockray & Aira Force Tearoom nearby.*

WALK 14
BY AIRA AND HIGH FORCE WATERFALLS TO DOCKRAY

As Aira Beck passes from Dockray to Ullswater it tumbles through a narrow wooded ravine via the delightful High Force and the spectacular Aira Force waterfalls. This anticlockwise circuit passes Aira Force and High Force via their east bank before climbing to Dockray and returning to the river by the west bank. Fine mixed woods, containing some magnificent ancient pine, plus the great 20m cascade of Aira Force, all fuse with the overall excellence of the surrounding countryside to make this a delightful outing.

THE ROUTE
Leave the car park, beneath the arch, and cross the field until the path leads right into the woods of the Lower Pinetum.

◆ Go right over the footbridge to cross Aira Beck and continue to follow the terraced track. Take the low route to gain the impressive view of the fall of Aira Force from the bottom bridge before climbing to the upper narrow stone arched bridge via the steps and hand rails. A stomach churning view down the falls and a slate memorial plaque to Cecil Spring Rice.

Approaching the village of Dockray.

◆ Follow the path up the east bank (true left) of the beck. A short deviation may be made by taking a wooden bridge which leads left, off the main path, to cross over a ravine and offer a viewpoint. Return to the main path and continue to the delightful rocky falls of High Force.

◆ Keep along the path and enter the little wood. Beyond the wood, fields lead easily to a junction of ways. Go left towards the building and enter Dockray directly opposite The Royal Hotel.

◆ Turn left down the road until, by the old quarry car park, a path leads off left (signpost 'Lower Pinetum'). Go directly down the field to the banks of the beck.

◆ Bear right to follow back down the west bank of the beck. The path leads down to overlook Aira Force and then through the woods of the Lower Pinetum before bearing right back to the car park.

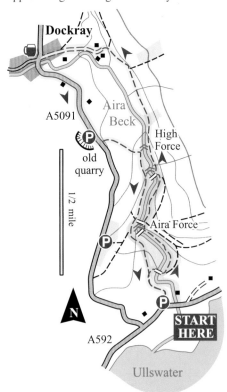

WALK 14

Aira Force and rainbow.

FACT FILE

CLASS: *Low Fell Walk (max alt 290m).*
LENGTH: 5 km.
TIME: 2 hours.
DIFFICULTY: *Mildly difficult on good paths (200m of ascent).*

START & FINISH: *National Trust Aira Force Car Park (NY 400 200).*
MAPS: *OS L90 or OL5.*
HOSTELRIES: *Aira Force Tearoom and The Royal Hotel, Dockray enroute.*

WALK 15
GOWBARROW FELL TRAVERSE

Starting from The Hause, the highest point of the walk, this walk makes a clockwise cir-cumnavigation of Gowbarrow Fell. The airy, easy, path above Ullswater is famed for its stunning views over all three legs of the lake and particularly those over the head of the lake to the high fells enclosing Patterdale. This is a journey contrasting the intrigue of the woods of Swinburn Park and the Aira Force Wood (Pinetum) with the openness of the lake and the quiet farms and cottages of Ulcat Row along Gowbarrow Fell's northern flanks.

THE ROUTE

Walk down the road towards Ullswater to pass a junction and find, near the bottom of the hill, a path signed 'To Aira Foirce', leading off to the right.

◆ Follow the path, narrow in places, but always well defined. After initial ascent the path traverses through the mixed trees of Swinburn Park. Beyond these cross a foot-bridge and ascend to pass through the stone wall.

◆ Follow the signed path leftwards and continue traversing towards the lake until a cairned viewpoint, below a stone bench, provides wonderful views over Ullswater. Keep traversing along the path and then de-scend to a point, before the woods, where a grassy path leads up to the right.

◆ Ascend the path to enter the woods above Aira Force. Keep right and then leave the wood to follow a path traversing first above and then back down into the wood. Continue along the good path to pass High Force.

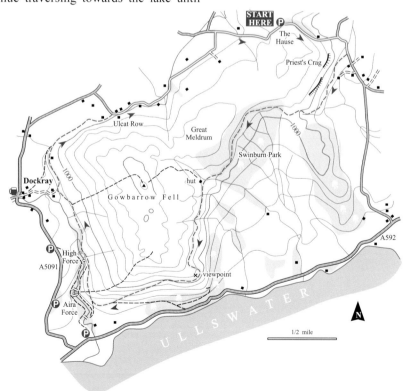

Looking to the head of Ullswater from the viewpoint below the stone bench.

Approaching the buildings of Ulcat Row.

Dockray.

◆ Before the house and bridge go right, signed Ulcat Row, and follow the path around to pass a cutting through a rocky knoll. Gain and follow the line of the stone wall continuing to pass farm cottages where the path becomes a track. Follow this to the houses of Ulcat Row

◆ Above the waterfalls the going opens only to enter woods yet again. Beyond the trees keep along the path pass through the stone wall and traverse the stone track towards the buildings marking the edge of and bear right along the surfaced road. Keep along this to a road junction and go right to climb the hill back to The Hause.

FACT FILE

CLASS: *Low Fell Walk (max alt 385m).*
LENGTH: *11¾ km.*
TIME: *4½ hours.*
DIFFICULTY: *Generally easy but with mildly difficult ascent (480m of ascent).*

START & FINISH: *The Hause lay-by (NY 423 235).*
MAPS: *OS L90 or OL5.*
HOSTELRIES: *The Royal Hotel Dockray and Aira Force Tearoom nearby.*

WALK 16
GREAT MELL FELL

From the A66 the independent hill of Great Mell Fell takes the shape of a great dome. However, on its far side, a tapering shoulder runs south eastwards from the summit. This provides a gradual and enjoyable route of ascent. The base of this shoulder is draped by mixed deciduous woods which soon give way to open fellside before the path traverses through a stand of Scots Pine. Beyond the trees the path opens again and ascends easily to gain the distinct summit. Great views extend to all points of the compass.

THE ROUTE
Leave the road and follow the lane passing a gate and stile to the second gate and stile on the right.

◆ Go through then take the path rising to the left. Ascend the path following along between the fence and trees.

◆ Beyond the thinning of the trees a distinct path climbs rightwards up the brackened felllside. Follow this rising to the shoulder and head leftwards ascending the shoulder to the wood of Scots Pine.

◆ Continue through the trees and follow the path beyond rising to the summit of the fell which is topped by the earthworks of a small prehistoric tumulus. Breathtaking views in all directions, particulary to Blencathra and the Northern Fells. Simply reversing the route of ascent offers a different aspect and provides pleasant, easy going.

Scots Pine wood.

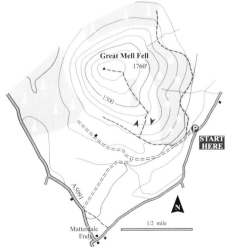

On the summit tumulus looking to the Pennines.

WALK 16

Great Mell Fell seen from Gowbarrow Fell to the south west.

Pony on Great Mell Fell.

FACT FILE

CLASS: *Intermediate Fell Walk (max alt 537m).*
LENGTH: *3½ km.*
TIME: *2 hours.*
DIFFICULTY: *Mildly difficult (280m of ascent).*
START & FINISH: *Roadside (NY 407 247).*
MAPS: *OS L90 or OL5.*
HOSTELRIES: *The Royal Hotel Dockray is nearest.*

WALK 17
DUNMALLARD AND MAIDEN CASTLE HILL FORTS

Surrounding the foot of Ullswater, as the high Lakeland fells diminish, there remains a fascinating landscape to explore. This walk, beginning directly from Pooley Bridge, climbs the now tree covered conical mound of Dunmallard Hill. Unsuspected from below, it reveals an Iron Age hillfort that once held sway over the surrounding countryside.Logically extending this walk leads over the tree clad hills and open fields surrounding Waterfoot to the earthworks of yet another Iron Age hillfort - that of Maiden Castle.

THE ROUTE

From the back of the car park take the track leading right, then climb the track which climbs steeply to the left. Continue up this, contouring rightwards, to gently ascend through the woods to a high point. With a small gate into the fields down to the right, go left to make steeper ascent directly up the earthy path ascending the north shoulder of the hill. Near the top it flattens and then breaches the upper bank of the Iron Age hillfort.

◆ Go south, through the trees, along the raised length of the fort, to descend the ramparts and gain the tree bedecked southern shoulder of the hill. The path is narrow but well defined and continues to make descent directly towards the lake (unseen through the mantle of trees). After a little way the path veers right slightly and joins the path which has circumnavigated the hill. Follow this to find in a little way a stile and then a gate leading off to the right (those wishing to return to the starting car park should keep left following the path circumnavigating the base of the hill).

◆ Head right along the path above the road and follow it to the junction. Cross the road and pass through gate between the stone gateposts. Keep left following parallel to the road to intercept a grassy trackway rising to the right. Ascend the track, passing the trees, to gain a fence line. At the outside corner of the fence head diagonally left

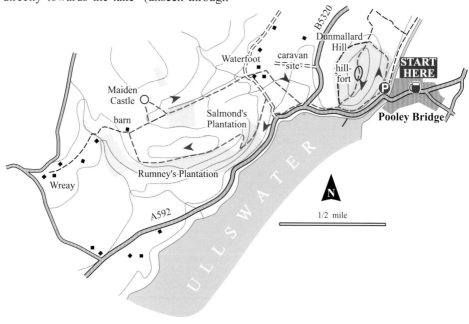

WALK 17

Tree clad Dunmallard Hill, ancient hill fort, rising above the foot of Ullswater.

ascending across the field to gain a further track. Continue left to find a wooden stile climbing onto the woods of Salmond's Plantation.

◆ Follow the narrow path through the trees ascending a stile over a fence. Go first right and then back left to follow along above the conifers of Rumney's Plantation. Climb over a couple of stride-over stiles which lead to a descent. At this point the path moves over diagonally rightwards, around the hillside, to another fence line and hedge. Continue along beside this, passing a concrete bench rest point, until at the bottom of the hill a gate leads rightwards to pass the end of a stone barn. This section can be badly churned by cows hooves and terribly muddy when wet.

◆ Beyond the barn follow along the hawthorn hedge first rising and then descending to a gate. Take the gate through the fence on the left. Climb beside the fence making grassy ascent to the faint earthworks of Maiden Moor.

◆ A path leads diagonally down the hill. Continue leftwards along the path, which has been upgraded, and then down beside the fence to find a gate at the bottom of the field. Go left along the road and then right into the Waterfoot Caravan Site. Pass the columns marking the entrance of the grand building then go right passed the end of the building. Go by garden and fountain, to find a gate into the fields. Continue across the fields to the gate between stone stoops leading to the road. Follow the path above the Pooley Bridge Road pleasantly back to the car park.

FACT FILE	
CLASS: *Low Fell Walk (max alt 270m).*	**START & FINISH:** *Car Park by Pooley*
LENGTH: *6 km.*	*Bridge (NY 470 245).*
TIME: *3 hours. (Dunmallard only, 45 min).*	**MAPS:** *OS L90 or OL5.*
DIFFICULTY: *Mildly difficult, the fields*	**HOSTELRIES:** *Plentiful in Pooley Bridge.*
can be muddy when wet. (320m of ascent).	

WALK 18
POOLEY BRIDGE BY LAKESIDE TO MOOR DIVOCK

An entertaining walk exploring the shoreline of Ullswater before ascending unspoilt fell-side to the prehistoric landscape of Moor Divock. Described in anticlockwise direction this walk traverses the lakeside continuing to pass a number of traditional farms before rising through the wild gorse to gain the trackway leading to the Bronze Age stone circle known as The Cockpit; this found, at the point at which the High Street Roman Road descends from the heights of the Eastern Fells. The views south over Ullswater to the mountains beyond are superb.

THE ROUTE

From the car park cross the bridge to the village of Pooley Bridge then immediately turn right down the driveway (public right of way). Go right and through the gate to the bottom of the lake. Follow the path along the lakeside continuing to enter the campsite of Hodgson Hill. Follow the track over the hill to pass the boat repair yard and reach the buildings of Waterside House Farm.

◆ Gain the road and turn right. Proceed along the roadway for 700 metres until, op-posite the Yacht Club, go left up the drive to Seat Farm.

◆ Go right by the first white building, then turn left and right again to walk along by the hedge to further building. Pass the build-ing and go left, by the corner of the garden, to follow rightwards along by the wall and through the fields to gain the buildings of Crook-a-dyke. Pass in front of this and continue along the track for 100 metres until a kissing gate and larger wood-en gate to the left give access to "PERMISSIVE PATH TOWARDS HOWTOWN AND MARTINDALE".

◆ Take the path lead-ing directly through the gorse bushes, boggy in places, and then head leftwards on the narrow path rising up the grassy fellside. In a short way this intercepts a well defined stony track unseen from below. Alternatively beyond the gorse take the path right-wards to the corner of Auterstone Wood to intercept the track at a lower point.

◆ Head left along the track ascending to the corner of Barton Park Wood. Keep along above the wall and make a short descent into a stony gorge. Take the path leading off to the right which contours the hillside to gain the low standing stones of The Cockpit Stone Circle.

◆ Descend the track to the left then rise to intercept the main route rising from Pooley Bridge. Go left descending this until gates

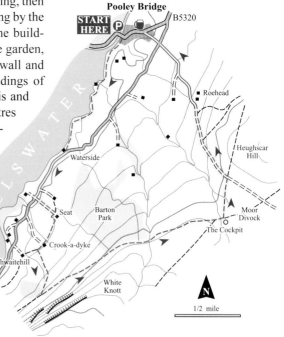

WALK 18

Looking back down the track, which rises to The Cockpit, over the last two legs of Ullswater.

big and small lead to the head of the sur-faced road. Descend the surfaced road, over the junction, down to the church of Pooley Bridge. Go left to finish.

Golden gorse above Crook-a-dyke.

FACT FILE

CLASS: *Intermediate Fell Walk (max alt 330m).*
LENGTH: *9½ km.*
**TIME:3 hours.*
DIFFICULTY: *Mildly difficult (270m of ascent).*
START & FINISH: *Car Park by Pooley Bridge (NY 470 245).*
MAPS: *OS L90 or OL5.*
HOSTELRIES: *Plentiful in Pooley Bridge.*

WALK 19
HALLIN FELL FROM MARTINDALE'S ST PETER'S CHURCH

Located strategically above the crook in the lake between the middle and last leg of Ullswater, Hallin Fell occupies prominent position. Its ascent from Martindale's St Peter's Church takes little effort yet offers wonderful views up and down the lake and also along the secretive valley of Martindale to the imposing heights of the High Street massif beyond. As described here an anticlockwise circuit, by first climbing above the head of the pass from Howtown, to reach the summit cairn is the most rewarding.

THE ROUTE

From the assorted roadside parking opposite the church take the grassy path ascending the hillside. After a short way take the path veering off to the right. Steep ascent leads to hilly tops above the bay of Howtown. These offer extensive views down the lake. Traverse along the grassy tops before veering left to climb the shoulder which leads directly to the 3m high rectangular masonry cairn adorning the summit of Hallin Fell.

◆ In descent pass the cairn, first heading westwards for a short way, then follow the distinct path south eastwards. This descends to follow beside the stone wall directly back to the road by the church.

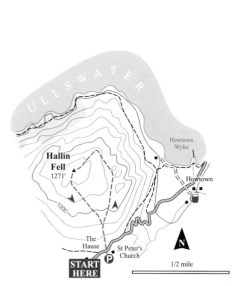

Daffodils by St Peter's Church in March.

Hallin Fell summit cairn.

Hallin Fell seen over Ullswater.

FACT FILE

CLASS: *Intermediate Fell Walk (max alt 388m).*
LENGTH: *2 km.*
TIME: *1 hour.*
DIFFICULTY: *Mildly difficult (155m of ascent).*
START & FINISH: *Parking near St Peter's Church Martindale (NY 436 192).*
MAPS: *OS L90 or OL5.*
HOSTELRIES: *Howtown Tearoom & Inn.*

WALK 20
THE MARTINDALE - FUSEDALE CIRCUIT
AROUND PIKEAWASSA

Starting by the characterful old church of St Martin's in lonely Martindale this route ascends and traverses the shoulder of Pikeawassa to gain the head of Fusedale. A distinct, now ruinous, stone barn stands at the head of Fusedale and marks the start of the grassy track which leads down into the delightful tiny hanging valley below. From the foot of the valley a good, gently climbing, track leads around the toe of the Pikeawasa shoulder, Steel End, and back over to Martindale. An excellent route by which to explore this lonely corner of the Ullswater area.

THE ROUTE

Ascend the road, with the St Martin's Church on your right, to gain the open fellside beyond. Take the distinct grassy path rising steeply to pass the high, ruinous, stone walled enclosure, to intercept the well defined narrow grassy track. (See alternative on the next page - MARTINDALE OVER PIKEAWASSA).

◆ Go right, contouring the flanks of Pikeawassa, to pass through a gate in the stone wall. Continue ascending the grassy track to the shoulder and stone wall rising over Brownthwaite Crag.

◆ The grassy track, well defined, keeps to the right of the summit and wall and gains the broad shoulder beyond before swinging back left to pass thorough a gap in the now ruinous wall. The path traverses the head of Fusedale to pass a small ruined building then a larger ruined barn.

◆ Continue traversing the hillside until the path becomes a better defined grassy track. Descend the track, pass a further ruined barn, and continue down Fusedale to cross a wooden footbridge over Dodds Gill. Take the track veering   left to cross the main Fusedale Beck by a further wooden footbridge.

◆ Keep on until in a little way a stone slab footbridge leads across the beck to the road. Go left down the valley road until, before the cattle grid, a track swings off the left.

◆ Gain and follow the track which contours around Steel End before making

gradual ascent to pass the high tiny Lanty Tarn.

◆ Keep on, passing the grassy track descending to St Peters Church, until a gate through the wall to the right, leads to a grassy path   around the hillside. Descend and pass below the front of the buildings of Cotehow. Continue to gain the track above the wall and go down this to the Martindale Road. Go left to the old church of St Martin's.

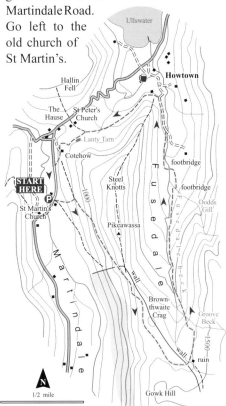

WALK 20

Start and finish by St Martin's Old Church, Martindale.

Dave Bishop descending Fusedale.

FACT FILE

CLASS: *Intermediate Fell Walk (max alt 430m).*
LENGTH: *6¾ km.*
TIME: *3½ hours.*
DIFFICULTY: *Mildly difficult (360m of ascent).*
START & FINISH: : *Parking by St Martins (Old) Church Martindale (NY 434 184).*
MAPS: *OS L90 or OL5.*
HOSTELRIES: *Howtown Tearoom & Inn.*

WALK 20A - ALTERNATIVE
FROM MARTINDALE OVER PIKEAWASSA

As per the previous route this walk ascends to the gate through the stone wall high above the old church of St Martin's but from here, not passing through the gate, it ascends directly to the high shoulder of Pikeawassa. The path on top of the shoulder heads north to the distinctive, blade-like, summit rock of Pikeawassa. With superlative views out over Ullswater descent leads along the shoulder of Steel Knotts and finally steeply down Steel End to the grassy track leading, above Howtown, from the botttom of Fusedale.

THE ROUTE

Ascend the road, with the St Martin's Church on your right, to gain the open fellside beyond. Take the distinct grassy path rising steeply to pass the high, ruinous, stone walled enclosure, to intercept the well defined narrow grassy track.

◆ Go right, contouring the flanks of Pikeawassa to reach a gate in the stone wall. Don't pass through the gate but climb directly to gain a narrow path running along the high shoulder above.

◆ Head left (north) along the shoulder and climb to the distinctive summit rock of Pikeawassa.

◆ Continue along the shoulder of Steel Knotts, which bears rightwards, to gain its steep terminus - Steel End. There are rocky sections and the going is quite exposed in places. However, steep descent is only short and it soon eases to gain the well-defined grassy track.

◆ Go left along the track, making gradual ascent to pass the high tiny Lanty Tarn.

◆ Keep on, passing the grassy track which descends to St Peters Church, until a gate through the wall to the right, leads to a grassy path around the hillside. Descend and pass below the front of the buildings of Cotehow (once an inn). Continue to gain the track above the wall and go down this to the Martindale Road. Go left to the old church of St Martin's.

Summit rocks Pikeawassa.

FACT FILE

CLASS: *Intermediate Fell Walk (max alt 432m).*
LENGTH: *4½ km.*
TIME: *2½ hours.*
DIFFICULTY: *Difficult, down Steel End*
only *(310m of ascent).*
START & FINISH: *: Parking by St Martins (Old) Church Martindale (NY 434 184).*
MAPS: *OS L90 or OL5.*
HOSTELRIES: *Howtown Tearoom & Inn.*

THE GRASMERE YEARBOOK

£26.00
Grasmere, at the heart of the Lake District National Park and World Heritage Site, is one of the most celebrated valleys in the region. Its character and beauty have made it world famous and inspired artists and writers for over two hundred years. This book is a personal photographic diary by award winning photographer Bill Birkett. All the four seasons, and their many moods, are represented and the photographic journey extends from lakeshore, through village, wood and meadow, to the high fell tops. Extensive captions are based on a lifetime's local knowledge.

The Grasmere Yearbook, signed by the author. Postage free (UK only) buy online from
www.billbirkett.com/shop